GIRLS' SportsZone

GIRLS' VOLLEYBALL

By Brendan Flynn

An Imprint of Abdo Publishing
abdobooks.com

abdobooks.com

Published by Abdo Publishing, a division of ABDO, PO Box 398166, Minneapolis, Minnesota 55439.

Printed in China.
102021
012022

Cover Photo: Shutterstock Images
Interior Photos: Pete Dovgan/Speed Media/Icon Sportswire/AP Images, 4–5; Petros Giannakouris/AP Images, 7; Rich Graessle/Icon Sportswire/AP Images, 9; Kyodo/AP Images, 11; Yuri Cortez/AFP/Getty Images, 12–13, 25; Kyusung Gong/AP Images, 15; Gwyneth Roberts/Lincoln Journal-Star/AP Images, 17; Manu Fernandez/AP Images, 19, 28–29; Tim Nwachukwu/NCAA Photos/Getty Images, 20–21; Yang Lei/Xinhua News Agency/Images, 23; Toru Hanai/Getty Images Sport/Getty Images, 30, 41; Frank Augstein/AP Images, 33, 35; Alessandra del Bene/Getty Images Sport/Getty Images, 36–37; Soeren Stache/picture-alliance/dpa/AP Images, 39; Dave Martin/AP Images, 43; Red Line Editorial, 44

Editor: Charlie Beattie
Series Designer: Jake Nordby

Library of Congress Control Number: 2021941591

Publisher's Cataloging-in-Publication Data

Names: Flynn, Brendan, author.
Title: Girls' Volleyball / by Brendan Flynn
Description: Minneapolis, Minnesota : Abdo Publishing, 2022 | Series: Girls' SportsZone | Includes online resources and index.
Identifiers: ISBN 9781532196386 (lib. bdg.) | ISBN 9781098218195 (ebook)
Subjects: LCSH: Volleyball--Juvenile literature. | Sports for girls--Juvenile literature. | Volleyball for girls--Juvenile literature. | Team sports--Juvenile literature.
Classification: DDC 796.325--dc23

TABLE OF CONTENTS

1

SERVING WITH APRIL ROSS

April Ross had history in her sights at the Olympic Games in Tokyo, Japan, in July 2021. The beach volleyball star had won a silver medal at the 2012 Olympic Games in London, England, with former partner Jennifer Kessy. She had won bronze in 2016 at the Rio de Janeiro Olympics with Kerri Walsh Jennings.

Now Ross was looking to add a gold medal to her collection. And she was looking to do it with yet another new partner. Alix Klineman didn't begin playing beach volleyball until 2017. She'd been a member of the US indoor team. But she switched to the beach after missing out on the 2016 Olympic squad.

Ross and Klineman paired up in 2018, and they quickly became a strong team. They took the silver medal at the 2019 World Championships. Their next major international competition was the Tokyo Olympics. There, the 39-year-old Ross and the 31-year-old

April Ross was a dominant server at the 2020 Olympic Games in Tokyo, Japan.

Klineman were favorites to win a medal. Ross wanted to make sure it was the right color to complete her set.

Serving Styles

There are two main types of overhand serves in volleyball. The easiest serve is a standing serve, or float serve. After a light toss, the server hits the middle of the ball with a short follow-through. The aim is to hit the ball with little or no spin so that it moves unpredictably. A topspin serve is more advanced. After the server tosses the ball in the air, she then hits the back of the ball near the top with her palm while flicking her wrist forward. The force of this forward rotation causes the ball to dip more quickly. These topspin serves also can be executed while jumping. The most advanced players also take a running start to their jump.

The Americans were facing a duo from Australia in the gold-medal match. It was 92 degrees Fahrenheit (33°C) at Tokyo's Shiokaze Park. Ross was serving early in the first set. She tossed the ball high into the air as she approached the back line. Then she leaped and delivered a powerful serve down the middle of the court.

The ball carried tremendous topspin as it rocketed over the net. Australia's Mariafe Artacho del Solar lunged to her left but could only get a glancing touch on the ball. The service ace gave the US team a 4–2 lead.

Ross, a five-time winner of beach volleyball's Best Server Award, went back to the line again. This time she buried

Ross, *left*, and partner Alix Klineman each earned their first Olympic gold medals in Tokyo.

an ace down the right sideline. The hard serve was well out of reach of either defender. All the Aussies could do was shake their heads. They had no way of predicting where the next serve would go.

Ross served two more points for the US. Klineman won them both with strong net play. The 7–2 lead gave the US team all the momentum it needed to win the match in straight sets. That day Ross served 25 times. She had four aces with only two service errors. Over the course of the entire tournament,

Ross was 156 for 169 (92.3 percent) on her serves. She had 15 aces in seven matches.

With the win over the Australian team, Ross finally had her gold medal. She was still in awe after the match. "I'm so in the present moment here with this team and this medal," she said. "I'm proud of my other ones, but just how this worked out, and the risk that Alix took to come on to the beach and her hard work . . . it doesn't happen without that."

Indoor Star

Most beach volleyball players don't start on the sand. The typical path to the beach begins with a background in indoor volleyball. April Ross was a four-year starter at the University of Southern California (USC). She started every match of her indoor college career and led the team in kills and points each season. Ross was a three-time all-American at USC. She then played indoors professionally from 2004 to 2006 before focusing on her beach career.

It All Starts with Serving

Serving is the way every rally is started. It is also the best way to control a match, whether on the beach or indoors. If a team can serve tough—meaning hard and accurate—it can put its opponent at a serious disadvantage. Sometimes that results in an ace. Or if an opponent struggles to control a serve, their first pass will be off the mark. That makes a set and spike more difficult to execute.

Ross won Olympic medals at three straight games with three different partners.

At the highest levels, coaches often form strategy around their best servers. In indoor matches, great servers are sometimes brought into the rotation just to serve. Coaches generally have an idea of the other team's strengths and weaknesses. So teams aim to send serves toward the players who have a more difficult time passing. This requires a great deal of skill by the server. Accurate serves are the mark of a good squad.

There are other strategies for serve location. A team might notice that the opposing setter struggles to get to the back of the court. In that case, the serving team might repeatedly serve the ball to that area. Or a server might try to catch the other team off guard by placing a ball just barely over the net. This type of deep and short serving is especially common in beach volleyball, where only two players are on a team. Another strategy is to serve the ball as hard as possible. Even the best players can struggle to control a hard-driven ball if it arrives more quickly than they expected.

Once the mechanics of serving are mastered, serving accurately is another test. Hard serves are especially challenging to keep in bounds. Veteran volleyball coach

QUICK TIP:
SERVE IT SOLO

Serving is one of the few volleyball skills that can be practiced alone. One way to practice serving is by setting up a target, such as a cone or a chair, on one side of the net. Then gather as many balls as possible on the other side. Use those balls to practice serving toward the target. After hitting it 10 times, move the target to another area and repeat. Serving might look like one of the simplest skills, but good serving requires accuracy. That comes from practice.

Haleigh Washington of Team USA keeps her eye on the ball as she lines up a serve during the 2020 Olympics.

Tom Peterson has some simple advice for those working on serving accurately. “Navigating the fine line between tough serves and missed serves is made easier by devoting due time and attention to working on the serve, both in and out of practice,” he says. That is the discipline and focus that helped Peterson become one of the best servers in the world.

2

DIGGING WITH JUSTINE WONG ORANTES

Women's volleyball debuted at the Olympics in 1964. Over the next 57 years, Team USA had often been a contender for the gold medal, but it had never won. The squad assembled for the Tokyo Olympics in 2021 was eager to finally change that.

The Americans won four of five matches in pool play, including a five-set thriller over Italy in their fifth match. The win clinched first place in Pool A. They then won their quarterfinal and semifinal matches in straight sets. A tough Brazil squad was all that stood between them and the gold medal. Brazil had beaten the United States for Olympic gold in 2008 in Beijing, China. They did it again in 2012 in London, England.

Team USA led 15–14 in the first set. But Brazil had scored three straight points. Justine Wong Orantes, Team USA's 25-year-old libero, had played very well all tournament. She was ready to get the Americans back on track.

Justine Wong Orantes digs a ball for Team USA during the 2020 Olympics in Tokyo, Japan.

Wong Orantes received a tough serve and passed it to setter Jordyn Poulter. Outside hitter Michelle Bartsch-Hackley smashed a spike attempt over the middle, but it was deflected. Brazil had a chance to set up its attack. A perfect set left Brazil's Fernanda Rodrigues open for the spike.

The ball rocketed toward the floor. But Wong Orantes shifted to her left, dropped to her knees, and made a clean dig. Poulter then tracked down her pass and set it for Jordan Larson, whose hard shot knifed through the defense for a point.

The Americans were closing in on victory in the third set. Leading 23–13, Poulter set up Larson for a spike. The Brazil blockers rejected the shot, sending the ball back over the net. Wong Orantes made a desperate dive for the ball. Using just her right arm, she deflected it to a teammate to keep the point alive. Team USA won the point and claimed the gold medal moments later.

Life of a Libero

Justine Wong Orantes was easy to spot. At 5 feet, 6 inches tall, she was the shortest player on the US Olympic volleyball team. She also wore a different-colored jersey than her teammates. That is because she was the team's libero, also known as a ball control specialist. The libero plays only in the back row. She cannot hit the ball while it is higher than the net and cannot set a ball in front of the attack line. But liberos still get plenty of action. Wong Orantes led the team with 82 digs in eight matches.

Wong Orantes's performance at the Tokyo Olympic Games earned her the Best Libero Award.

Those key plays were the result of Wong Orantes's skill and experience. While the Tokyo Games were her first Olympics, she had already helped the squad win two Volleyball Nations League gold medals. In 2021 she was named the league's top libero. Wong Orantes capped off her great year with a gold medal and another Best Libero Award in Tokyo.

Against Brazil, Wong Orantes showcased great positioning and quick reactions. Both are important against opponents with strong attackers. Perhaps most important, however, was Wong Orantes's technique. Over years of practice, she knew how to delicately dig the ball so that it would stay in play. A bad dig could send the ball flying or force her teammate to make a difficult set. But a careful dig can pave the way for an accurate set and a powerful attack.

Receiving Strategy

As teams become more advanced, coaches may decide that only a few players receive serves. The most common strategy is a five-player system. This is where everyone except the setter is responsible for a certain area of the court. In a four-player strategy, two players cover the right side (one in front, one in back), and two players cover the left side (one in front, one in back). If a coach decides to have only three receivers, one would cover the left side, one the center, and one the right.

Receiving and Digging

There are three primary types of passes: the serve receive, the set, and the dig. The serve receive and the dig are similar. They both keep the play alive. The serve receive and dig also both lead to a set. A good set leads to a better attack. That is how teams win matches.

The serving team has the first opportunity to set the tone for a rally. The serve receive is the opposing team's first opportunity to change the tone and take control. A good serve receive passes the ball to the setter. The setter then sets the ball for another player to attack. The first goal for a serve receive is to keep the ball in play. After that, the second goal is to get the ball to a teammate as accurately as possible.

Former US national team setter Courtney Thompson drops down for a dig during a 2016 match against Puerto Rico.

Mike Hebert was the women's volleyball coach at the University of Minnesota from 1996 to 2010. "A quick offensive tempo begins as a concept on the coach's clipboard," he said. "It can become reality only if the team can pass accurately."

Once a rally begins, digging is often the best bet to keep it in motion. Digging is when a player stops an opposing spike or attack from touching the ground. It is similar to a serve receive.

One difference is that a spike usually comes from the opposing frontcourt. That means the ball can come in at sharper angles and at faster speeds. At the highest levels, defensive players have only a split-second to react to a hard-driven spike.

Digs and serve receives are usually executed with two arms out in front of the body. The goal is to contact the ball with the inside of the forearms. However, a player might not have time to get in position. Sometimes players need to dive to reach a quickly falling ball. Or players might only have time to stick out an arm to try to make contact. If a player keeps the ball off the ground and gets it to a teammate, the rally continues.

A good passer needs to have visual, physical, and mental skills. The player's eyes need to see the ball well. She must watch from the moment it leaves the opponent's hand until it arrives on her own forearms. A player's footwork helps her

QUICK TIP:
FLAT FOREARMS

To get a feel for how your arms should be held when passing, hold a board that is 8 inches (20 cm) wide by 10 inches (25 cm) long. Each hand grabs a top corner, with the sides of the board against the forearms. Lock your elbows. This is how stiff the arms should be. Bring the hands together when playing an actual match, but visualize the arms being as stiff as that board.

Wong Orantes jumps into the arms of teammate Haleigh Washington after Team USA knocked out Serbia in the Tokyo Olympic semifinals.

get in position to receive the serve. Her arms must absorb the contact while sending the ball back into the air.

A good passer also must have confidence. This comes from hours of proper practice. She must have the ability to forget any mistakes from the past. In volleyball it is common for a team to serve at a player who just made an error. That person might continue to make mistakes if she cannot get the bad play out of her mind.

3

SETTING WITH JORDYN POULTER

As Team USA's setter, Jordyn Poulter rarely receives a serve. When the ball is served, she quickly races from her spot in the rotation to the center of the court, just a few feet from the net. Then she immediately turns her body toward the ball. She knows the first pass is coming her way. Poulter then decides who gets to attack. Her decision must be made in an instant.

Poulter decides while she positions herself under the ball. As it falls, she positions her body so it is square with where she wants to pass. Then the ball is on her fingertips for a split second before it is sent toward her attacking target.

Poulter straightens both arms as she completes the set. If she wants the ball to go forward, she rounds her back and follows through in that direction. When she wants it to go backward, she arches her back and follows through. If the pass only needs to travel a few feet, Poulter simply flicks her wrists in the

Jordyn Poulter sets up a University of Illinois teammate during the 2018 national semifinals.

direction she wants it to go. When her intended attacker is on the front line, Poulter aims her pass to fall a couple feet off the net. For a back-row hitter, her pass falls a few feet in front of the attack line.

In Team USA's second match of the Tokyo Olympic Games in July 2021, Poulter was in control. The opponent was China, the defending Olympic champions. Early in the first set, Team USA's 24-year-old setter received a pass from libero Justine Wong Orantes. She had teammate Haleigh Washington charging the net in front of her. But she also knew Jordan Thompson was attacking the net behind her. Poulter connected with Thompson on a back set, and Thompson buried a spike for a point.

Later, the first set was tied at 26–26. The first team to 25 points wins, but that team must win by two points. Neither China nor the United States could pull away. Then Poulter

The Comeback Kid

Before she could claim every Olympian's dream of a gold medal, Jordyn Poulter suffered an athlete's worst nightmare. In the final pool match against Italy, Poulter suffered an ankle injury when she landed on a teammate's foot. The injury looked potentially serious. Fortunately, Poulter missed only one match. After sitting out the quarterfinals against the Dominican Republic, she was back in the lineup. She barely missed a beat. Poulter had 32 assists against Serbia in the semifinals. She added 36 more against Brazil in the gold-medal match.

Poulter led the United States in assists at the Olympic Games in Tokyo, Japan, and was named the tournament's best setter.

and Thompson teamed up again. Poulter settled under a high pass from the back row. She flicked another back set, and Thompson crushed it again. Team USA won the point and went on win the set 29–27. The Americans eventually won the match in straight sets. Poulter finished with 51 assists.

Poulter also helped the Americans get out to a fast start in the finals against Brazil. Leading 3–0 in the first set, the teams had a long rally. Finally, Poulter found herself with a clean chance to make a set.

She had options. Michelle Bartsch-Hackley, the team's leading hitter, was approaching on the left. Annie Drews was in position to the right. And Washington was circling around Poulter for a short set up the middle.

Instead, Poulter surprised everyone. She directed the ball back toward the attack line. Jordan Larson charged in from the back row and tipped the ball over the net. The unexpected move caught the Brazil defenders off balance, and the ball fell for a point.

The United States went on to win their first Olympic gold medal with a 3–0 victory. Poulter had the most assists of any player in the tournament and won the Best Setter Award.

Faults

One of the most common faults called on setters is the double hit. This occurs when one hand contacts the ball before the other. The hands must remain evenly spaced until the ball leaves the fingers. Another common fault for setters is a lift. This is when the player holds the ball too long. If a player tries to set the ball from either too low or too high, she is more likely to lift or carry the ball.

Setting and the Setter

By definition, a set is a pass in which the ball is positioned for a teammate to attack. That makes it very important in any volleyball match. A well-placed set helps the attacker make a good shot. Setting also involves a lot of strategy. The setter must constantly be aware of

Poulter, *left*, and teammate Annie Drews take a bite out of their gold medals after beating Brazil in the Tokyo Olympic final.

her surroundings. Which teammates might be ready to attack? Where are they? Where are the opposing players lined up? When a team scores a point on a powerful spike, there was usually a good set just before.

There are a few different ways to set up a teammate. The most basic method is the forearm pass. This also is called a bump set. It is often used at the youth levels. Bump sets are common when a team's first pass is too low for the setter to do an overhead set. Forearm passes are common in beach volleyball. The two beach players have a lot of ground to cover. They are not always able to get under a ball for an overhead set.

The overhead set is the most common type of pass at the high school level and higher. This is when the player softly lifts the ball up using her fingertips. A player can be more accurate using her fingertips rather than her forearms. Ideally any set will leave the ball a few feet off the net. That allows the attacking teammate to follow through on an overhand swing without touching the net.

The most important part of the setter's strategy is getting the ball to one of her team's best attackers. Those players are often based on the far sides of the court. The setter must keep the defensive players in mind too. If the direction of a set is too obvious, opposing players can get in a better position to block the ball.

One way to keep opponents guessing is by using a quick set. This short pass goes to the player closest to the setter. It requires precise timing because the attacker does not have much time to judge the flight of the ball. Another tricky play is the back set. This is when a setter passes the ball behind her without looking at a specific player.

The best teams do many things to try to disguise attacks. Often multiple players will begin attack approaches even before the set. That gives the setter several options to pick from. It also means the opposing blockers cannot key in on one potential attacker.

The setter is one of the most important players on the floor. She must be accurate and alert. In a split second, the setter must decide where to place the ball and then physically send it there. It takes a lot of hard work and practice to reach Poulter's level. But having a good setter can be the difference between a good team and a great team.

QUICK TIP:
STRENGTHEN THE FINGERS

To develop stronger fingers and improve setting, try doing wall pushups on your fingertips. Stand about three feet (0.9 m) away from a wall. Then extend your arms until the fingertips touch the wall. Let your weight fall forward, then push yourself up from there. As you become stronger, hold a ball against the wall and push up off the ball. Stronger fingers will help you better place the ball while setting.

4

SPIKING WITH JORDAN THOMPSON

Heading into the Tokyo Olympic Games, Jordan Thompson was emerging as one of Team USA's top attack threats. The 6-foot-4-inch outside hitter graduated in 2019 from the University of Cincinnati, where she set a record with 6.27 kills per set. She made her first appearance for the US national team that year and helped the squad clinch an Olympic berth.

Once the Olympic Games began in Tokyo in July 2021, it didn't take long for Thompson to demonstrate why she was considered a rising star. The Americans were facing China, the defending Olympic champions. China opened the match with the serve. Team USA libero Justine Wong Orantes received it and delivered a soft pass to setter Jordyn Poulter. Thompson began moving forward from the back row. Poulter placed her set back toward the attack line. Thompson exploded into the air. She swung her right arm and hammered a spike through China's defense for the first point of the match.

Jordan Thompson shows off her incredible leaping ability against Turkey during the 2020 Olympic Games in Tokyo, Japan.

Thompson goes up for a spike against Turkey during the Tokyo Olympics.

Three points later, the same trio teamed up again. This time, Thompson raced up the left side of the court to receive Poulter's set. At the peak of her jump, she struck the ball down with the palm of her right hand.

The kill attempt deflected off the hands of a Chinese blocker and landed out of bounds for another US point. It was one of many dominant moments for Thompson, who finished the match with 28 successful kills on 50 attempts. By comparison, the rest of the US team combined for 30 kills on 82 attempts. This followed Thompson's performance in the opening match against Argentina, when she went 18-for-23 on the attack. "Jordan Thompson has become a world-class weapon so far in this tournament," said TV announcer Paul Sunderland.

Thompson was well on her way to winning the Best Spiker Award when she was injured in the Americans' fourth match of the tournament. Attempting a block, she landed on a teammate's foot and rolled her ankle. The severe sprain kept Thompson on the bench for the rest of the Olympics. However, Team USA went on to win the gold medal despite missing their top outside hitter.

Thompson finished the tournament with 66 kills in 119 attempts, an amazing 55.5 percent success rate.

Hooker the Jumper

Former Team USA star Destinee Hooker's height (6 feet, 4 inches) made her an ideal attacker. But her jumping ability set her apart. As a track star at the University of Texas, she won the college high jumping title in 2009. A year earlier she nearly qualified for the Olympic Games in high jumping. She placed sixth at the Olympic Trials but needed to be in the top three. Hooker could jump 43 inches (109 cm) off the ground and reach up to 11 feet, 2 inches (3.35 m). That is almost 4 feet (1.2 m) higher than a women's volleyball net at 7 feet, 4 1/8 inches (2.24 m) high. With her height and jumping ability, she could often hit volleyballs over a block. She helped Team USA win the silver medal at the 2012 London Olympics.

No other player finished the Olympics with an efficiency rate higher than 41.4 percent.

Mastering the Spike

Spiking is the most exciting play in volleyball. It is the one skill that every young player wants to learn. But it is often the most difficult skill to master, because it combines accuracy and strength. It is also a high-risk, high-reward play. It can immediately give your team a point if the spike lands in. But it can immediately give the other team a point if it lands out or in the net. Opposing teams also can take momentum if they block a spike.

For great athletes like Thompson, spiking involves jumping high above the net and smacking the ball toward the other team's court. The best attackers can jump very high. That allows them to drive the ball down with lots of power and at a tight angle.

Stepping Up

Annie Drews was a first-time Olympian when she suited up for Team USA in Tokyo. The 27-year-old native of Elkhart, Indiana, did not expect to play much with Jordan Thompson holding down the opposite hitter position. But when Thompson went down with an ankle injury, Drews stepped up. After little playing time in the first three matches, Drews led the team in kills in each of their last four contests. She had an incredible 21 kills in the quarterfinals and added 14 more in the decisive gold-medal match.

Before an injury knocked her out of the Olympic tournament, Thompson had 66 attack points in just four matches.

Spiking is an advanced skill, though. Most young players learn how to execute a standing spike from 15 feet (4.6 m) behind the net. In doing this, the player tries to hit the bottom third of the ball with the palm of her hand. Then she finishes by snapping her wrist forward and pointing the fingers down. This creates topspin on the ball. Topspin makes the ball dip in flight, so it is harder to dig.

With practice and growth, players can begin spiking closer to the net. Eventually players add an approach and jump. But even the best players still sometimes use a standing spike in games. A player might not be able to make a good approach for a jump.

Players also can attack using off-speed hits. The roll shot is one example. It is carried out like a regular spike until the hitter eases up just before making contact. Instead she softly hits the ball with an open hand over or around the blockers. The key is to make it look exactly like a spike until the last moment.

Another off-speed hit is the open-handed tip. It is similar to the roll shot, but contact is made with the pads of the fingertips instead of the palm. The ball generally will not travel as far as a roll shot. An open-handed tip can take advantage of the empty space right behind the blockers. It is a touch shot that should

QUICK TIP:

ONE-ON-ONE DRILL

To practice hitting, grab another player and stand at the attack line on either side of the net. Together you can play a one-on-one game. One player starts by tossing or serving the ball to the other. The partner then makes three contacts and sends it back over. Each player can pass and set to herself. Then work on the different types of hits: tips, roll shots, and spikes. Begin by performing each shot 10 times while standing, then do the same while jumping.

Annie Drews led Team USA with 14 attack points in the 2020 Olympic gold-medal match against Brazil.

just barely go over the blockers' hands and fall to the floor before any other defenders can reach it.

These off-speed shots are especially effective in beach volleyball. The defensive player in the back will often creep toward one side. If the attacker notices, she can poke the ball to the other side. Or if the back defender stays on one side, the hitter can attempt an open-handed tip to land immediately behind the blocker.

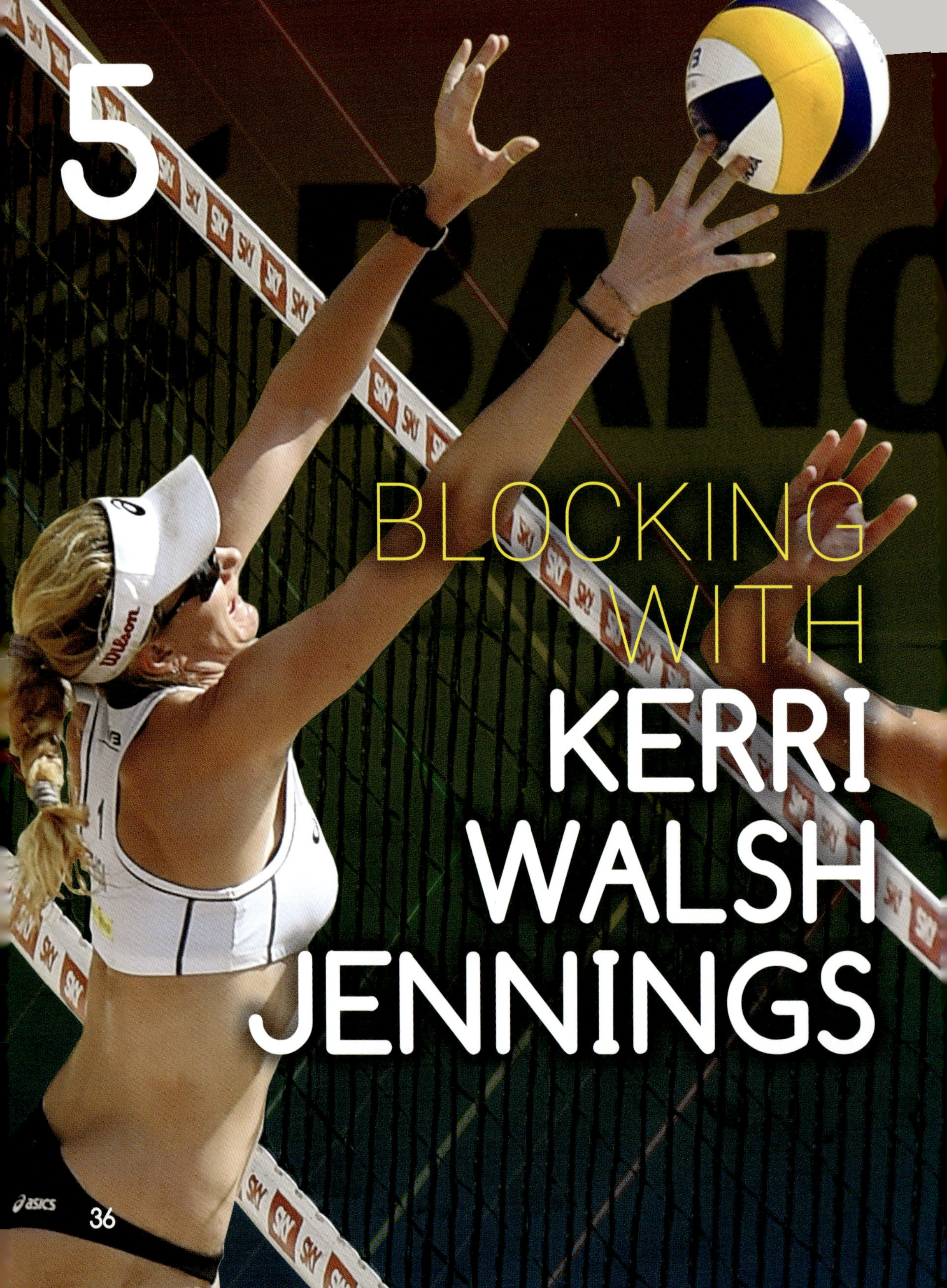

5

BLOCKING WITH KERRI WALSH JENNINGS

Kerri Walsh Jennings entered 2016 Olympics in Rio de Janeiro, Brazil, looking for her fourth straight gold medal in beach volleyball. It was not to be, however. She and partner April Ross were upset in the semifinals. But they still had a chance to go home with a bronze medal.

Walsh Jennings is thought by many to be the greatest beach volleyball player of all time. The 6-foot-3-inch Californian partnered with Misty May-Treanor to win gold at the 2004 Olympic Games in Athens, Greece. They repeated the feat in 2008 in Beijing, China, and 2012 in London, England. But while May-Treanor retired after the London Games, Walsh Jennings forged ahead with Ross.

Walsh Jennings and Ross were facing the Brazilian team of Larissa França Maestrini and Talita Antunes da Rocha for the bronze. Brazil took the first set. In beach volleyball, the first team to win two sets wins the match. The Americans had a steep hill to climb.

Kerri Walsh Jennings executes a block at the 2008 Olympic Games in Beijing, China.

The Americans turned the tables and won the second set. To win the third set—and the bronze medal—Team USA needed to reach 15 points first with a two-point lead. With the Americans leading 13–9, Walsh Jennings rose to the occasion.

Alix Klineman

Kerri Walsh Jennings has long been considered the world's best beach volleyball blocker. That title might have been passed to American Alix Klineman in 2021. The 6-foot-4-inch Klineman played indoor volleyball until 2016. But she failed to make the Team USA roster for the 2016 Rio Games. The next year she moved to the beach full-time. She was a quick study. Klineman won the Best Blocker Award on the top US beach volleyball tour in 2018 and 2019. Then in 2021, she and April Ross cruised to the gold medal at the Tokyo Olympics. They lost just one set in seven matches, often with Klineman dominating play at the net.

Larissa looked to set up Talita for a kill on the left side of the court. Walsh Jennings positioned herself at the net and prepared for a block that could all but seal the match. She bent her knees as she watched the flight of the ball. Then she threw her arms straight up and jumped.

Talita made good contact on the ball, but Walsh Jennings got both hands on it. As she finished the block, she bent her hands slightly forward to make the ball bounce down. It shot straight into the sand for a 14–9 lead.

Walsh Jennings, *left*, rises up to stop Brazil's Talita during the bronze-medal match at the 2016 Olympics.

Ross served for the match. Larissa's return pass set up Talita for another kill. Once again Walsh Jennings was right there. This time the ball came off her hands with backspin and shot to her left. Larissa's desperate dig attempt couldn't save the point. Walsh Jennings's two straight blocks won the third and deciding set for the American duo.

Blocking: The First Line of Defense

A volleyball team with strong offensive players is likely to score a lot of points. Of course, teams that score a lot of points win a lot of matches. But a good squad needs its defense to score too, and that means blocking. Whether on a two-person beach volleyball team or a six-person indoor volleyball team, blocking is a key aspect of any game.

Blocking stops an opponent's shot from crossing the net. The goal is for the block to send the ball to the opponent's court for a point. Sometimes teams that get blocked can save the play and continue the rally. Blocks are often very sudden, though. That makes the opposing team more likely to make an error. Blocking shots can also frustrate opponents and build momentum for your team.

Blocking an opponent's shot involves timing, strength, and anticipation. A blocker first must watch the ball as the other team receives it. As the ball is set, blockers need to judge where it will come down. The quicker they can get to that spot, the better. This takes good side-to-side movement.

Stuffing the Stat Sheet

Defense played a huge role in the United States' run to indoor volleyball gold at the 2020 Olympic Games in Tokyo, Japan. The US team had 84 total blocks in the tournament and had more than their opponents in six of their eight matches, including all three knockout-round matches. As expected, middle blockers Haleigh Washington and Foluke Akinradewo led the way. Akinradewo finished with 21 successful blocks, while Washington added 20.

Foluke Akinradewo, *right*, and Jordyn Poulter, *left*, dominated defensively for Team USA at the 2020 Olympic Games.

To cover a short distance, blockers side-shuffle their feet while keeping their hands near their shoulders and their bodies facing the net. This side-to-side movement becomes more important when a team needs more than one player to block at a time. The blockers must move together.

A blocker must first get to the spot where her opponent is hitting. Then the blocker plants her feet and squats. Squatting helps the blocker jump high. The goal is to jump straight up. The player must be careful to not let momentum carry her into the net or into a teammate.

As they jump, the blockers straighten and raise their arms and spread their fingers wide. The idea is to cover as much space as possible. The blocker tries to reach the highest point of her jump when the opposing attacker hits the ball. The arms should face slightly downward so that a ball hitting them would

QUICK TIP:
FOOTWORK IS KEY

Blocking definitely takes skill. However, positioning is just as important. There are some easy ways to improve your side-to-side movement. One drill requires either a coach or a teammate to help. Have your partner stand on a chair on one side of the net, about two feet (0.6 m) in from the sideline. Stand directly across the net. When your partner spikes, attempt to block it. Upon landing, sidestep to the near sideline, then sidestep back to the original position. Your partner then spikes again as you jump. Upon landing this time, crossover step toward the far sideline. Then crossover step back to the starting position.

Walsh Jennings, *right*, finished her Olympic beach volleyball career with four medals, including three golds won with her longtime partner, Misty May-Treanor.

be sent toward the ground. It is also important to keep the arms stiff because the force of a hard-driven ball can otherwise bend them backward. That could allow the ball to pass through.

Blocking might not be used as often as skills such as serving, passing, setting, and digging. However, as Walsh Jennings has proven, a team that can block is a team that is incredibly hard to beat.

COURT DIAGRAM

ATTACK LINE

A line on the floor that runs parallel to the center and end lines on both sides of the court. It is 9 feet, 10 inches (3 meters) from the net and separates each side into a front zone and back zone.

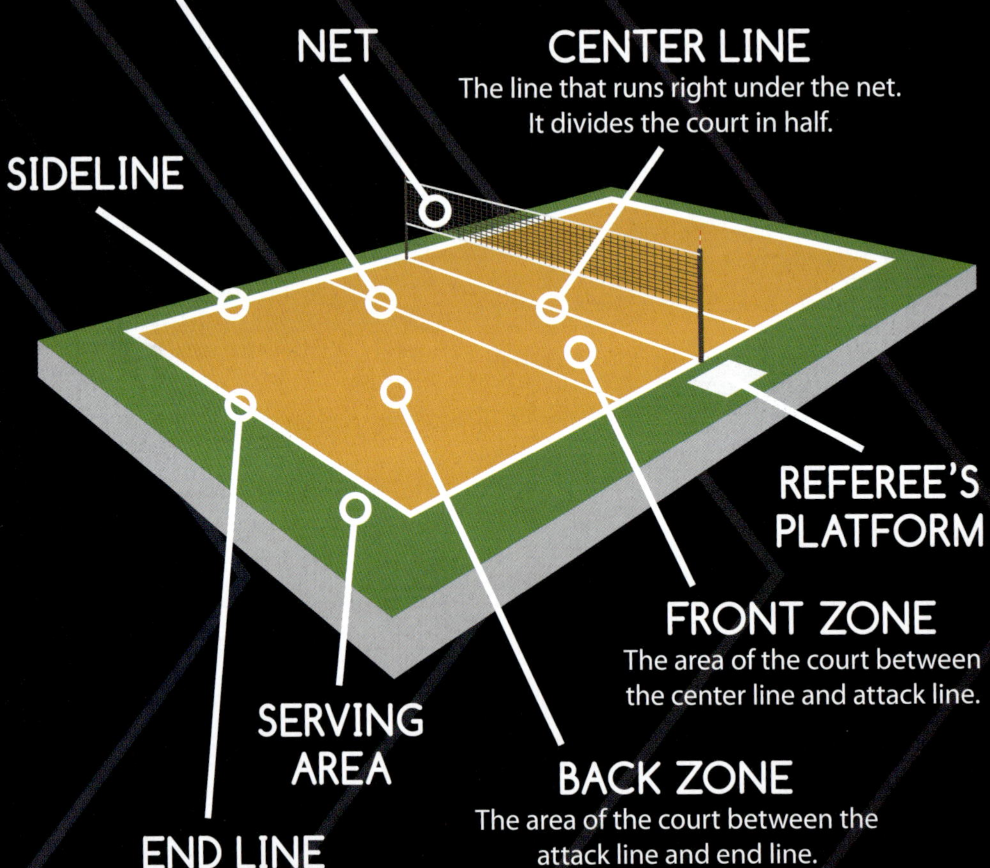

CENTER LINE

The line that runs right under the net. It divides the court in half.

FRONT ZONE

The area of the court between the center line and attack line.

BACK ZONE

The area of the court between the attack line and end line.

END LINE

The line at either end of the court that connects with the sidelines. Serves must be taken from behind the end line.

GLOSSARY

ace

A serve that lands in the opponent's court, scoring a point for the serving team.

approach

The movements a player makes prior to jumping and hitting the ball.

assist

The pass that comes immediately before a teammate successfully attacks.

attack

An attempt to score a point by hitting the ball over the net toward the opponent.

dig

A pass that stops an opposing attack from hitting the ground, usually using the forearms with the hands together.

lift

When the ball comes to a stop in a player's hands. This is also called a hold.

rally

The series of actions two teams make to keep the ball in play.

rotation

The act of an indoor team's six players moving from one position to the next in clockwise fashion. When a team earns a serve, each player moves one spot.

spike

A hard-driven ball from a player's overhead swing that lands in the opponent's court.

MORE INFORMATION

BOOKS

Ackerman, Jon. *Make Me the Best Volleyball Player.* Minneapolis, MN: Abdo Publishing, 2017.

Evdokimoff, Natasha. *Volleyball.* New York: AV2, 2020.

Monnig, Alex. *Total Volleyball.* Minneapolis, MN: Abdo Publishing, 2017.

ONLINE RESOURCES

To learn more about women's volleyball, please visit **abdobooklinks.com** or scan this QR code. These links are routinely monitored and updated to provide the most current information available.

PLACES TO VISIT

US Olympic & Paralympic Museum

200 S. Sierra Madre St.
Colorado Springs, CO 80903
719-497-1234
usopm.org

Opened in July 2020, this unique museum showcases Olympic and Paralympic history and is situated near the US Olympic & Paralympic Training Center in Colorado Springs. The museum features several interactive exhibits, including sports demonstrations, a simulated parade of nations, and a complete set of replica Olympic Torches from 1936 to the present

Volleyball Hall of Fame

444 Dwight St.
Holyoke, MA 01040
413-536-0926
volleyhall.org

Learn about the greatest athletes to ever play the game of volleyball—in the town where the game started. The Volleyball Hall of Fame opened in 1987, and its first inductee was the late William G. Morgan, the inventor of volleyball. The Hall serves as a living memorial to the sport.

INDEX

ABOUT THE AUTHOR

Brendan Flynn is a San Francisco resident and an author of numerous children's books.